Letterland

ELT

Hello! I'm Monkey.
What's your name?

My name is

_____

Sounds

Children colour the things that start with Clever Cat's 'c...' sound.

Numbers 1 2 3

Children count the cats and colour the correct number on the right.

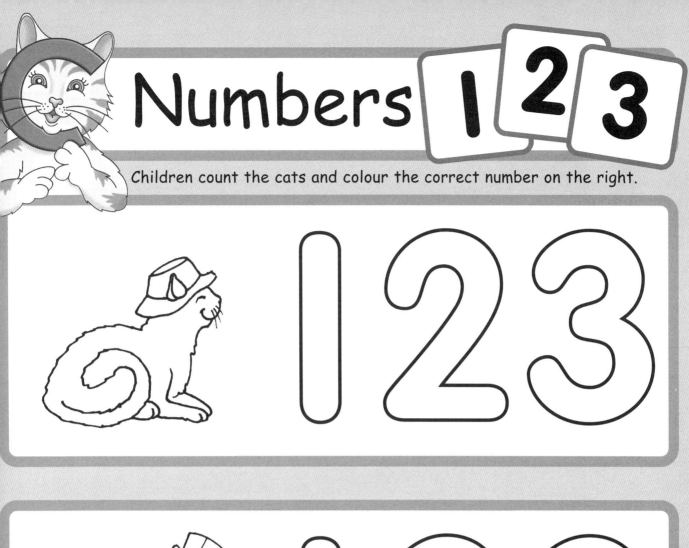

Sounds

Children circle the objects that begin with the Letterlander's sound.

Numbers

Colour these apples red. Count the apples and colour the correct number on the right.

Colour this apple yellow.

Colour these apples green.

Sounds

Children circle the object that starts with the target sound.

6

Numbers

Write over the numbers then say them aloud with a partner

Match the numbers to the ducks.

4

5

6

7

7

Sounds

Children circle the letter that matches the first sound of each word.

h a h c h d

  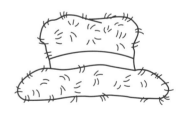

h d h a h c

Numbers **8** **9**

Write over the big numbers. In pairs, count the hats and houses aloud.

9

Sounds

Circle the picture that starts with the Letterlander's sound.

		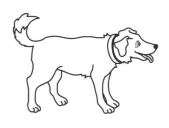

Numbers

Write over the numbers.

1 2 3 4 5 6 7 8 9

Circle nine mice. Take turns to show a partner nine mice, counting aloud. ("1, 2, 3, 4..." etc.)

Sounds

Circle the objects in each row that start with the Letterlander's sound.

  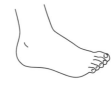 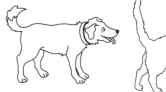

Numbers

Write over the numbers in numerical order.
Count the fingers on a partner's hand.

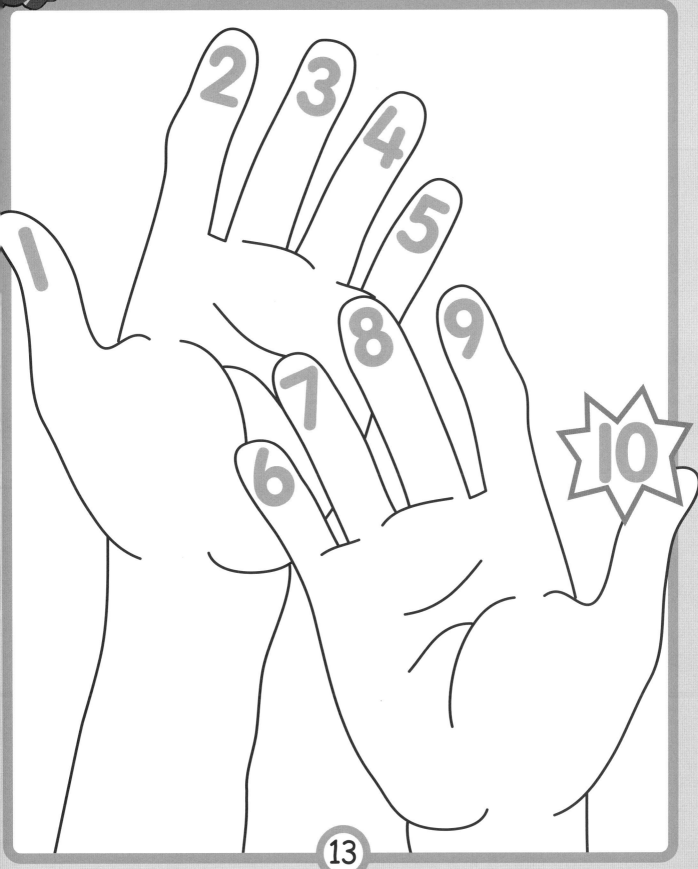

Sounds

Circle the objects that start with the target sound.

c	
a	
d	
h	
m	
t	
s	

Happy faces

In pairs count the objects aloud. Draw a happy face if the number matches the pictures. If it doesn't match, write in the correct number.

 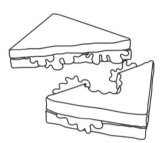 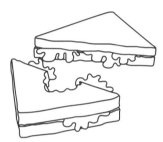 

 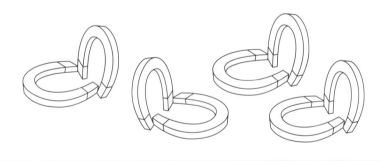 

 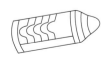 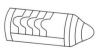 

Sounds

Circle the object that starts with each Letterlander's sound.

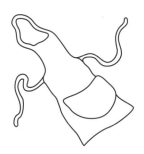

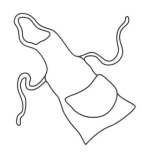

Colours

red | blue | green

Colour each leg a different colour.
Student A points to a leg: "What colour is it?" Student B: "It's red!"

17

Sounds

Circle the things that start with the Letterlander's sound.

Numbers 1 2 3

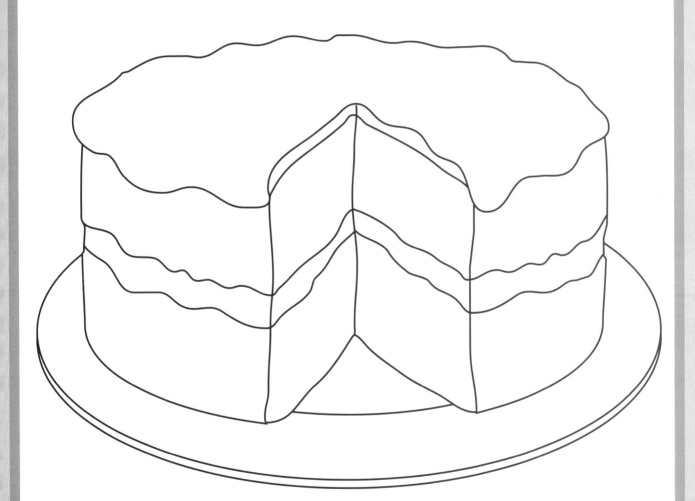

I am ___ years old.

Sounds

Circle the object that starts with the Letterlander's sound (short vowels) or name (long vowels). E.g. 'old man' starts with Mr O's name.

  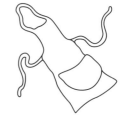

Shapes & colours

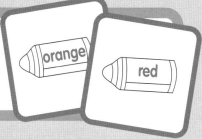

1. Help children to colour the shapes below.
2. Give Student A cut-outs of two red squares, two red triangles and two red circles.
   Give Student B two orange cut-outs of each shape.
3. Students fill in their grids by asking for the missing shapes, "Please give me a (red) (square)."
4. Children swap cards and play again.

red

orange

red

orange

red

orange

 # Sounds

Which Letterlander's sound starts each word? Circle the letter.

d c

a i

d t

h m

n m

10

t d

s c

a i

9

m n

a o

d p

p t

People

Colour in the picture and give each person a name.
Introduce every person to a partner. "His name is...", "Her name is...".

23

Sounds

Which Letterlander's sound starts each word? Write over the correct letter.

y   g

y   g

y   g

y   g

Big or little?

Children colour the dinosaur and grapes green. Colour the sun and apple yellow.
In pairs they play a riddle game. "It is little and green. What is it?" etc.

25

Sounds

Which Letterlander's sound starts each word? Fill in the correct letter.

 _____

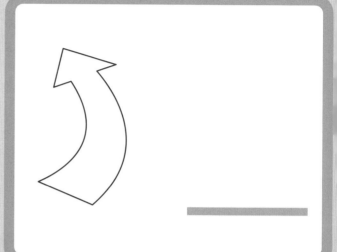 _____

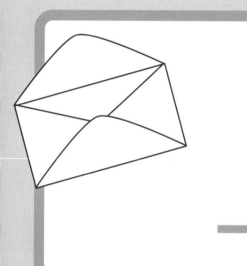 _____

 _____

 _____

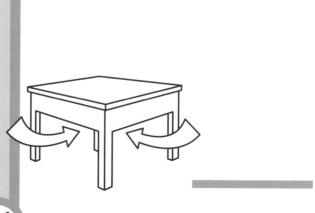 _____

Picture-code

Add Uppy Umbrella to her letter in the word **sun**.
Add Eddy Elephant to his letter in the word **ten**.

sun

ten

Sounds

Which Letterlander's sound starts each word?
Fill in the correct letter.

Draw & say

Draw the things that start with each letter in the correct column.
Students take turns to say, " I am Kicking King. I start words like..." etc.

Kicking King

Clever Cat

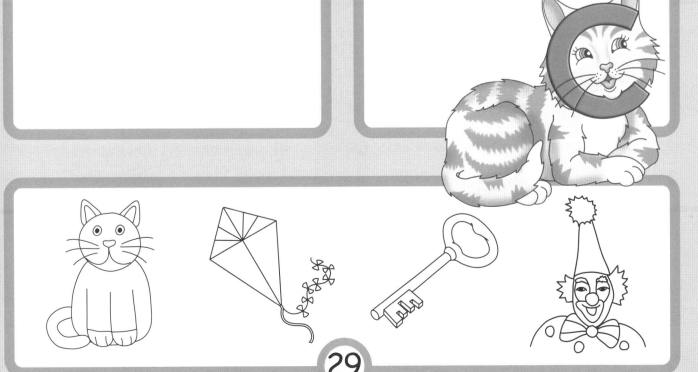

29

Sounds

Join each Letterlander to his or her favourite food.
Student A: "I like to eat cake. Who am I?" Student B: "Clever Cat!"

Favourite food

Firefighter Fred's favourite food is fruit.
Ask, "What do you like to eat?" Children draw their own favourite food.

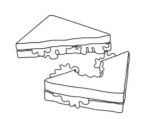

Sounds

Circle the object that begins with the Letterlander's sound.

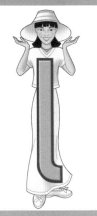

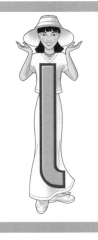
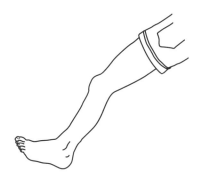

32

Rooms

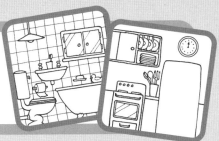

Student A points to a room. Student B says the name of the room: bedroom, living room, kitchen or bathroom. Then they swap roles.

33

Sounds

Join the Letterlander to the object that starts with his or her sound.

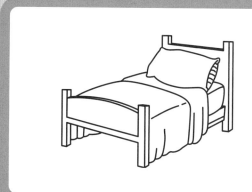

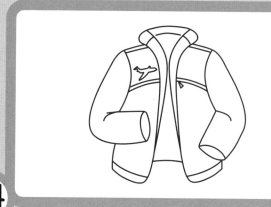

34

Animal game

Student A mimes one of the animals.
Student B guesses the animal and points to it. "It's a duck!"

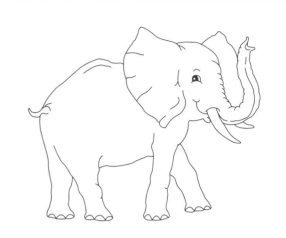

35

Sounds

Circle the letter that matches the first sound.

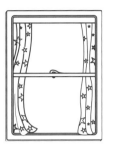

w   v   y

v   w   x

y   w   x

Sounds

Draw a happy face if you can hear Max's "k-ss" sound at the end of the word. Draw a sad face if you can't.

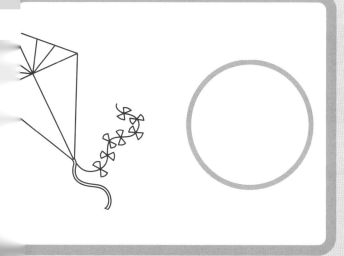

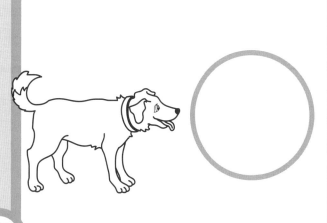

Sounds

Colour the things that start with Zig Zag Zebra's sound

Sounds

 sh

Children write 'sh' to complete these words.

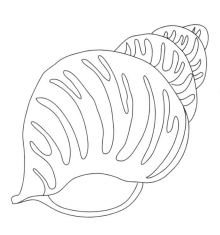

_ _ _ell

_ _ _ip

spla_ _ _

fi_ _ _

Sounds

Children write 'ch' to complete these words.

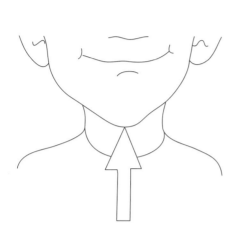

__in

__ick

__ildren

ben__

40